DO WHAT YOU LOVE

Essays on Uncovering Your Path in Life

by
Henri Junttila

Table of Contents

Introduction 5
How to Read This Book 10
On Not Knowing 13
On Having Too Many Ideas 18
On Wasting Time 24
On Thought 29
On Sharing Your Truth 37
On Criticism 43
On Opportunity 49
On Challenges 55
On Uncertainty 61
On Overnight Success 67
On Practice 73
On Making Money 79
On Running Away 85
On Synchronicity 90
On Finding Your Path 96
On Getting Started 102
Final Words 107
A Request 110
Books 111
Connect 112
Resources 114

Introduction

Doing what you love is not a new concept. It's been around for thousands of years. The name, the label, may have changed, but the essence of it has not.

Two thousand years ago, Socrates had what he called a daemon, an inner voice that guided him through life. Goethe had a similar thing—a voice within that compelled him to fulfill his destiny.

Likewise,

Even in Rumi's popular poems you will find passages such as: "Let yourself be silently drawn by the strange pull of what you really love. It will not lead you astray." *this life vs? next life?*

Doing what you love means listening to what makes you come alive. Listening to your own inner guidance. ~~It means knowing that~~ you have certain strengths and preferences. ~~And it means using~~ those to craft a life worth living. *use*

Dismiss the calls ~~from your soul~~, and you ~~risk feeling~~ empty, depressed, lost, and confused. I know, because I've been there.

This applies to every human being on this planet. We all have access to a deeper part of ourselves, ~~waiting~~ to nudge us in the right direction. Throughout the ages, this has been called by various names: Intuition, instinct, God, subconscious, heart, wisdom, and so on.

It doesn't matter whether you want to do work you love, or if you want to pursue a hobby. This book isn't about a system, or a formula—it's about pointing to the wisdom within you waiting to guide you through life.

in order

gently with one's elbow,

Prod sb with a finger, foot, or pointed object to draw their attention to something

6

I'm a pragmatic person.

I thrive on logic.

When I first discovered the path of following my heart, I didn't quite believe it. I didn't think simply following my interests would make a difference. But I had no other choice. I was miserable. I thought, "Why not give it a shot?"

I did.

And my life changed.

The more I've begun to trust my inner guidance, the happier I am, and the smoother life is. This doesn't mean I'm problem-free or fearless, because no one is. It just means that I know how to navigate life.

The results?

More joy, happiness, fulfillment, passion, and fun.

Deep down, you know this. But you hear conflicting advice. People saying to not do what you love. To be practical. Get a job. Take the safe path.

The fact remains that no one knows you better than you do, which means that it is not until you begin listening to yourself that your life begins moving in the right direction.

correct

So this book isn't about me telling you what to do. This is about me sharing what I know, and what I've learned from helping thousands of people through my books, courses, and website: WakeUpCloud.com.

This isn't a theory, *only on paper!*

This is how I live my life.

serendipity

Once I began following this path, it was as if life began cooperating with me. Some call this coincidence. Some call it synchronicity. All I know is that it happens. *the simultaneous occurance of events which appear significantly related but have no discernible causal connection.*

When I was willing to face my fears, and dive in, everything changed. Doing what you love may seem impossible, but it's not.

8

As you continue reading, you'll notice what's been holding you back, and you'll feel lighter and more at peace. You'll realize that you have what you need to start. And you'll uncover the only thing that ever stood in your way.
↳ no less, if not no more!

How to Read This Book

This book was born out of the questions I get from my readers, customers, and clients. Since 2009, I've helped people find and follow their passion, to do what they love.

it's not vs. it is $\square$ it isn't

During that time, I've noticed that doing what you love isn't complex. It's extremely simple. But simple doesn't always mean easy. Sometimes the simplest things are the hardest.

Guan Ning keeping at his work!

What I write about comes from my personal experience. I wasn't born knowing what to do.

10

I had to learn this the hard way. There were no books for me to read, because I didn't know that this was possible.

Yet somehow I found my way.

I listened to my interests, and I put one foot in front of the other. *true interests which are universal! true interest vs. empty temptations*

I have focused each chapter on one problem. You can read each chapter as a stand-alone essay. However, I recommend that you read the book from beginning to end, as it has threads woven through it.

At the end of each chapter, you'll find an action step, where I invite you to either think about a specific question, or explore it via writing. Doing this will help you make this information your own.

You may notice that I use the terms 'do what you love,' 'passion,' and 'purpose,' interchangeably. They all mean the same thing to me, which is to follow the magnetic pull of life.

You may also notice that I repeat certain concepts from time to time. This is by design. When you find that a concept is repeated, pay attention. Let it sink in.

Remember, you may not find everything you read to be useful. That is how it should be. Take what feels good to you, and use it. Discard the rest.

This is about you.

Not about me.

On Not Knowing

When you embark on your journey toward doing what you love, you're putting together a puzzle. But this is no ordinary puzzle. You find pieces here and there. You're often confused, because you have no idea what this puzzle is supposed to look like.

As you start finding your path in life, you have a puzzle to put together, but you won't know what it looks like until you create it. You have to experiment, and feel your way through.

The good news: Figuring out where you're going is not your job. Your job is to do what you can

How one knows what they can or can't do?

with what you have. In other words: To follow your excitement, your heart, your wisdom, or whatever you want to call it. Everything doesn't have to make sense. Not right now.

Following your heart means noticing what you feel pulled toward. You are unlike anyone on the planet, so you have to forge your own path. You have to tap into your own wisdom.

All you have to do is get out of the way. In other words, stop taking your thoughts so seriously, and stop trying to figure everything out. Because when you relax, your inner wisdom shines through, and the pieces of the puzzle begin falling into place.

When I started following my heart, I didn't know what to do. But I quickly realized that the problem wasn't knowing what to do; the problem was being willing to start before I *thought* I was ready.

As Kamal Ravikant, author of *Live Your Truth*, writes: "The best people, they're afraid, they question themselves. Many, if you corner them, will admit that they wonder if they're good enough. But what separates them from the rest is that they jump off the cliff anyway. Sprout wings on the way down." *faith?*

My problem was the idea I had about doing what I love. I thought I had to have it all figured out before I started. I thought I needed a plan, an idea for a breakthrough product, and a revolutionary message. Turns out I needed none of those things.

I needed the courage to start.

To act.

To experiment.

Sounds simplistic. But it worked for me.

Sometimes the simplest advice is the best. The problem isn't the simplicity, but the willingness to apply what you learn.

There is a time for contemplation, but if you're paralyzed and confused, that time has passed. Looking for answers in a mixed up mind is not a recipe for success.

So what if, just what if, this isn't about knowing, but about starting?

Whatever ideas you have about doing what you love, let them go. Notice that they are thoughts you choose to give power to. If your definitions hold you back, throw them in the trash.

Start experimenting.

Look at the interests you already have, no matter how insignificant you think they are.

And above all, don't take this too seriously. The more you relax and the more fun you have, the more your inner wisdom says hi. It has always been there, waiting for you. When you stop analyzing and planning, it emerges.

If you truly feel like you have zero interests, zero passions, the solution remains the same: Get moving. What's stopping you is *thinking* that you need to pick the right thing. Thinking that you lack something.

As you do your best with the puzzle pieces you have, the picture will become clearer and clearer.

16

But in order for that to happen, you <u>have to start with the pieces you have.</u> _→what do I really have or do I really lack ◦what I assumed?_

Start with the interests you already have.

Do your best, and see where life leads you.

Action Step

In each chapter of this book, I'll end with an action step. You can do these action steps in your head. But I recommend you use good old pen and paper.

For this chapter, I want to invite you to look at how you hold yourself back from starting. What thought do you believe that stops you from moving forward?

Then ask yourself: If I didn't believe this thought, what would my next step be?

When you're ready, I'll be waiting for you on the next page.

On Having Too Many Ideas

Before I began seriously listening to my inner wisdom, I was afraid of failing, and of humiliating myself. This kept me from taking a more playful approach to life. I was so serious that it was sucking my soul dry.

I had notebooks filled with goals, dreams, and ideas. I had visualized what I wanted my life to be. But it never went anywhere, because I wasn't willing to test my ideas in the real world.

As Ray Bradbury once said: "Life is trying things to see if they work."

The problem wasn't having too many ideas, but being unwilling to test them. I get emails all the time from people who have a laundry list of passions and skills. Yet they're stuck. Because they're trying to figure it all out before they start.

What I've discovered is that trying to figure things out gets in the way of clarity. When I started my blog, Wake Up Cloud, I didn't know if my idea was going to pan out. I didn't know if anyone would show up. But I decided to start anyway.

Why?

I wanted to.

want only works & is of sacred value only if the I is .....? (fill the blank)

When I thought about the idea of starting a blog, I felt open, free, and curious.

I had held myself back for years, because I wasn't sure about where I was going. A day came when I was sick of trying to figure things out, and I just started.

Once I started, I had an aha moment: I realized that all I had to do was act on my excitement from moment to moment. All I had to do was follow my heart, my wisdom, as best as I could. I didn't have to know where the path would lead.

But we know our start and our End. So we know it in truth, just the forms hidden.

What I had to do was test the ideas that inspired me. Not all at once, but one at a time. I had to let go of trying to analyze things to death, and act on my inner nudges.

→ but there are two of such! Always two in opposition. Which to follow? Or act & adjust?

At first, the idea of starting a blog didn't set my heart on fire. But it felt magnetic, and I wanted to explore it to see what would happen.

You may not have one passion—or one idea—grabbing you by the throat. You may simply have an interest in something. This interest is a seed that grows when you give it attention, when you take action and explore it further.

So the problem for me wasn't having too many ideas, too many passions, but being unwilling to take action. Once I saw this on a deep level, I noticed that all I had to do was pick one idea that felt good, take action, and do my best.

As I watered my blog with attention, it grew.

I listened to my audience and to my inspiration.

I received feedback.

And I course-corrected.

seemingly not perfect

You have to be willing to pick the wrong idea. You have to refuse to stand still. It's okay to stumble forward, to fall, and to *not* know what you're doing.

You can always come back to other ideas if one doesn't work out. But if you never test your ideas, you'll never know what they could've become.

Charles F. Kettering, businessman and inventor, once said: "Keep on going and the chances are you will stumble on something, perhaps when you are least expecting it. I have never heard of anyone stumbling on something sitting down."

Inventors, entrepreneurs, and creators of all kinds all fail more than they succeed. What makes them successful is their willingness to keep going despite both internal and external resistance.

So remember, the fact that you have too many ideas means that you have a wildly creative mind. It's a matter of where you focus your superpower. Use your mind to test your ideas in the real world. It is only through taking action, and exploring the ideas you have, that you will gain clarity.

Just because you have too many ideas doesn't mean you can't take action.

It may seem like you can't, but you're always one thought away from taking the first step.

Action Step

Grab your pen and paper, and explore the following question: What's an idea that you're capable of taking action on, and that you feel curious about?

Just for now, put aside any doubts, and entertain the idea. How could you take action on it?

Remember to think small. Think tiny. For example: Instead of trying to write a book, write one paragraph in one chapter. Instead of trying to build a popular website, write one article.

It is through tiny steps that your dreams are achieved. We'll keep coming back to this concept of tiny steps throughout this book.

On Wasting Time

When you're starting out doing what you love, or any new project, you've probably noticed the fear that your efforts will prove to be all for nothing. Or that you'll make the wrong decision and waste years of your time.

This becomes a problem because it makes you waste time right now. The thought says that if you take action, you might end up wasting time, when in reality you're wasting time now.

There's also the assumption that you know what is worth doing, and what is not. If you're honest with yourself, you can't know. None of us know what's going to happen, or how things will turn out.

Haven't you ever done something that you thought was a waste of time, but turned out to be a blessing in disguise?

And on the flip side, haven't you ever done something that you thought was worth doing, but turned out to be a waste of time?

We can't know what the future holds. All we can do is live life one moment at a time.

For example, many of the mistakes and failures on my path have led me to look in different directions, and uncover roads that I didn't see before. *There are ethical issues which if disregarded, in proportion to how much of violation has been committed, that is a malignant waste of time.*
The truth is that I don't know what will be a waste of time, and what won't. As far as I know, nothing I do is a waste of time, not even wasting time. The reason is because I learn from everything, even when I think I don't.

Even if I write a book that no one reads, I will have gained something through the act of creating the book, and thinking deeply about a topic. I will have learned what didn't work. And the sheer act of taking action will inspire further action. I hope so!

So when you think you're going to waste time, you're actually wasting time right now. You're stuck in your own thinking, and you feel bad.

A sage is Calm, and not subject to external forces!

The fact that you're feeling bad is a sign from your wisdom that your thinking cannot be taken seriously.

Beneath not wanting to waste time is wanting to get somewhere. Somewhere that will make me happy, and make things okay. I might have a goal of doing work I love. I believe that the goal will make me happy, so now I want to waste as little time as possible, because I want to get to my goal, so I can be happy.

There's another assumption hidden there. A big one. Can you spot it?

It's the assumption that something outside of myself can make me happy. Yet that's never the case, because happiness comes from the inside.

I don't know about happiness's overflow from the inside or what the author is 26 referring to by "happiness", but if it means the emergence & cultivation of something worthy from within that one can rely upon amidst hardships, I too agree.

My thoughts determine how I feel. Not life. Not circumstances. I'm always feeling my thinking.

This assumption also covers up the fact that at my core, I am already happy and at peace. Have you noticed that when you stop thinking, you're happy, or at least content? That's because we all have what we need. We just have to get out of our own way.

If you want to do what you love, you have to be willing to step outside of your comfort zone.

Once you do, you'll see that your fears and worries hold no power over you.

As long as you're doing your best, and learning from your mistakes, you're growing. And growth is never insignificant. It's never a waste of time.

You may go down a path that looks like a failure on the outside, but on the inside it may teach you something that changes your life forever.

Whatever you may think of the future doesn't change what you need to do right now. It always comes down to doing what you can with what you have, and following your inner wisdom.

If you waste time, so what?

Who says you have to take life so seriously?

Do what you can with what you have.

That is enough, because it's the only thing that's possible.

Action Step

No pen or paper required for this action step.

I want you to close your eyes, and think of a time when you were in flow. When you were relaxed. And when you thoroughly enjoyed life.

Notice the outlook you had. Become aware of how you related to your thinking. Bask in this feeling for a moment. Enjoy it.

When you're ready, the next chapter awaits.

On Thought

So far, we've touched on how it's not life holding us back from anything, but our thoughts. Or in other words: The thoughts we entertain.

You see, you are the creator of your experience. I'm not talking about you creating your reality and circumstances. I'm talking about how you experience life. Everyone experiences life through their thoughts.

For example, my pet fear is about money. So when something that I perceive to be bad happens, I project out to the future, and I feel horrible. Traffic to my blog might dip. I might get a 1-star rating for one of my books. When this happens, my mind assumes that it's the beginning of the end.

Meanwhile, in reality, no catastrophe has occurred. It's all going on in my head. I'm feeling my thinking.

You are always feeling your thinking. You don't feel your circumstances. Circumstances happen, a thought pops up, and you feel something.

You don't have to control your thinking, nor do you have to change your thoughts. All you have to do is notice how your experience is created.

In my case, simply noticing how I'm creating my experience helps. It doesn't feel as close. I know that it's just my thinking. When I don't try to fix it, it eventually returns to normal. I bring my attention to the present moment, and if something needs to be done, I'll do it.

When you feel frustration, anger, confusion, or any negative thought, it's a signal from your inner wisdom that your thinking cannot be trusted. You don't have to do anything about it, because your thinking will return to normal if you don't get in the way.

As Lao Tzu once said: "Muddy water, let stand, becomes clear."

The same is true for your mind. When you don't try to figure things out, things figure themselves out. We're taught that we have to make things work, when in fact we aren't in control.

Take a look at your life, and some of the major events. Maybe you met a loved one, you got a great idea, or something else happened. You had no control over any of those.

Our job is not to control life. Our job is to experience it fully.

So what does this have to do with doing what you love?

Everything.

It's never life getting in the way of you doing what you love, but your thinking. Or I should say, the thoughts you choose to entertain.

This doesn't mean that you never have bad moods, but simply that you don't take your thinking too seriously.

Now, this isn't always easy. Sometimes I have days where my head is filled with worry and fear. During those days, while I may be in a low mood, I know that it's my thinking, so I don't act on it. Not as much as I used to.

Now you might ask, "But surely there are times when my thoughts are helpful?"

Of course.

When you feel lighthearted, free, peaceful, and joyous. That's when you're most in touch with your heart and your inner wisdom. That's the time to solve problems, and make decisions.

When you feel negative, you often feel a sense of false urgency. You start fixing problems that don't even exist.

When it comes to doing what you love, there's nothing you have to do, except get out of your own way. Excuses, fears, and worries are thoughts. They seem real, because that's how life works. But seeming real doesn't make them real.

It's like going to the movies. It seems real. Sometimes you even forget that you're watching a movie. But it isn't real. The same is true for how we create our experience of life.

As you stop trying so hard to figure life out, you start gaining clarity. You can see this for yourself. Look at your life, and notice where you have the best ideas and solutions. It's when you're walking, taking a shower, on vacation, reading, or doing something that relaxes your mind.

When your mind relaxes, your inner wisdom shines through. We're all part of something bigger. At the molecular level, we're all made of the same stuff. There are no boundaries between you and me, even though it feels that way.

Now, I don't want you to blindly believe what I say. I encourage you to challenge these ideas, and to experiment with them.

Find out for yourself.

Notice how you're always feeling your thinking. Life is never making you feel anything. You don't feel your circumstances. You don't feel life. You feel your thoughts.

As Michael Neill writes in his book *The Inside-Out Revolution*: "No matter how scary or oppressive or insecure your experience of life may be, once you realize that it's only your own thinking that you're experiencing, that thinking loses much of its hold over you."

And that's how I experience my financial fears. They may feel real to me, but I know that it's my thinking. I know that the best I can do is to be in the present moment, and do what I can with what I have.

So if you're feeling down, notice that it's your thinking doing that. Take a walk. Watch a movie. Let your thinking return to its normal state of calm.

There's nothing you have to do (mentally).

Your heart, your wisdom, is always there, waiting for you, because that's what you are at your core.

You are happiness, joy, excitement, and all of the things you've been searching for. It may not feel like it, but as you keep moving forward, you'll uncover more and more of it.

Action Step

For this chapter, all I'd like you to do is to notice how you are always feeling your thinking.

You don't feel circumstances. You don't feel life. You feel your thoughts. Your thoughts give you your experience of life.

Set aside one minute to do this now.

On Sharing Your Truth

Do you feel like you don't have anything special to offer the world? And if you had something to offer, that no one would pay you for it?

You may be interested in spirituality, personal growth, or even business. You may have insights to share, but you stop yourself because of fear and doubt.

And even if you overcome your fear, there are people out there who know more than you. You can't compete with them, can you?

Well, what if you could?

When you get out of your own way—when you have one of those days where you feel great—do you feel that you have something to offer?

The answer is yes, isn't it?

Even if it's a tiny yes, it's still a yes. You see, deep down you know you have something to offer. But if you're feeling down, your feeling (and thinking) will give you a different experience of the world.

Still, you may feel like what you know is mundane. You might wonder, "Isn't this obvious? Doesn't everyone already know this?"

The answer is yes and no. The people you can help don't know. Or they don't know your perspective. There's a reason there are thousands of websites and books on the same topics.

The reason is because we're all unique. Not one single person is the same as another. No one has your experiences, or your worldview.

When I started following my heart, I knew I wasn't the best out there on personal development. But I also knew that this was what I yearned to do. I had two options: To give in to my fears or to take action anyway.

For me it came down to the fact that it didn't matter if there were others out there. Or if what I had to share was too simple. What mattered was the fact that I wanted to do it. That was enough.

Deep down, you can feel yourself being pulled in a certain direction. What's holding you back are the thoughts you entertain. I keep repeating this for a reason: Once you see that you're always feeling your thoughts, your life changes.

When your head clears, you feel optimistic about life. That's a sign from your being that you're on the right track. When you're bogged down with thoughts of trying to figure things out, you feel bad, because it's a sign that you need to take a step back and take a break.

The fact that your thoughts change with your mood only shows that your thoughts are more illusionary than you've thought until now. Just because you think you have nothing to offer doesn't make it so.

This doesn't mean people will flock to you and praise whatever you do. It simply means that you can start with what you have.

You can learn.

You can improve.

The better you get, the more people you can help. And the more you help, the higher the likelihood that you can make money doing what you love.

There are no guarantees. No magic formulas. No secrets. Just the willingness to start with what you have, where you are.

And remember, what's obvious to you may not be so obvious to someone else. I'm constantly surprised at how much of an impact my words have. Yet I often feel like I'm simply sharing the obvious. You see, I get caught up in my thoughts as well. I'm not immune. I do my best, and I keep sharing my truth.

It's enough. You are enough.

You have something to offer, otherwise you wouldn't be reading this. We're all a part of a larger tapestry. I don't know how, or why, but that's what I've noticed.

So let your thoughts go crazy. Let your fears try to convince you to stay put. But you keep putting one foot in front of the other. Keep taking tiny steps. Keep listening to your wisdom. Because when you do, you realize that you do have something to offer.

Don't try to be like someone else.

Be who you are.

That is enough.

That is why you're here. That is what your heart aches to do.

As Rumi said: "Respond to every call that excites your spirit."

Action Step

When you're feeling good, inspired, excited, and uplifted, how do you feel inspired to help the world?

Answer this question when you're feeling good.

Remember, when you feel good, trust your thinking. When you feel bad, take a break.

On Criticism

When you're afraid of putting yourself out there, you're afraid of what people will say. You're afraid of being judged, being exposed as someone who doesn't know enough.

It doesn't matter whether you're a singer or a writer; a coach or an engineer—when you share what you think, you're putting yourself out there. It could be putting your writing online, speaking up in a meeting, or telling your friends what you really think.

Instead of being yourself, and sharing your ideas, you may feel the need to hide behind a mask. To stay quiet in hopes that no one will judge you. If you do this, you're already judging yourself.

You don't have to pretend to know more than you know. You don't have to pretend to be someone else. People are drawn to you because of your story. Because of your perspective.

You will never know everything. There will always be more to learn. People will always have an opinion about what you do, whether you put yourself out there or not.

We want approval, and we always will. But we don't need approval from everyone. You don't have to please everyone in the whole world. And you can't. There will always be someone who doesn't like what you do.

When you share your truth, the right people are attracted to you. But put on a mask, and people will be attracted to a false image, which will leave all parties unsatisfied.

You never have to claim to know more than you do. People crave real people with real stories. You know when someone is putting on a show.

You're smart. You can tell when something is off. But what happens when someone exposes themselves to the world, scars and all?

How do you react?

If the person has the same struggles as you, you feel closer to them, because you've heard their story, and you can relate to it.

To transcend the fear of putting yourself out there, notice that it's a story you tell yourself. A thought you believe. It's not that you're actually afraid of putting yourself out there. You're afraid of the thought of putting yourself out there.

Let that last paragraph sink in.

Don't try to figure it out.

Thinking about this isn't going to solve your problem. You know this because you've already tried that path. As William Clement Stone said: "When thinking won't cure fear, action will."

As you take action, the fear diminishes, because you begin to see through your thoughts. You notice that you were already experiencing your own criticism by imagining the worst that could happen.

Your fear is telling you that you will feel bad if you put yourself out there, but you're already feeling bad thinking about it, aren't you?

I've seen this first hand as I've stretched my comfort zone. And I'm not alone; popular blogger and best-selling author James Altucher wrote in a blog post: "I don't hit "Publish" unless I'm scared."

We all struggle with putting ourselves out there. You're not the only one. The reason most people don't share their story is because of fear.

To free yourself from the shackles around your heart, you have to realize that what you think and feel isn't always true. Realize that the shackles never existed in the first place.

I've written thousands of articles, been interviewed, written books, and created courses. I've been criticized. People have questioned me.

And I've come to realize that no amount of criticism in the world can touch me.

I alone determine how I feel by the thoughts I entertain. Don't get me wrong. I still wince when someone says something bad about me. But this isn't about getting rid of the initial reaction, but about the reaction to the reaction.

I wince. But I don't have to think about what it means. I don't have to analyze my fear, to get rid of it, or do anything special.

In the end, I can only put out my story. I can only do my best. (I keep repeating this for a reason).

People crave what you have to share.

But you have to be willing to take the first step.

Action Step

This action step is a three-part question:

1. What are you truly afraid will happen if you put yourself out there?

2. Can you be absolutely sure that that's going to happen?

3. And even if it does happen, can you know that it's going to be negative?

Grab your pen and paper and answer the questions above. It'll only take a few minutes.

I'll be waiting on the next page.

On Opportunity

I spent most of my life believing that I couldn't draw. Then one day in the summer of 2012, I decided to join a cartooning course.

I spent the next year and a half sketching on a daily basis. I went from stick figures to colorful cartoons. But more than that, I realized that I could change.

As I learned to draw, I began seeing the world differently. The sky was no longer blue, but different shades of blue with a splash of green.

During sunset, I could see yellow, orange, red, blue, green, and other colors. I saw trees in a new light, observing how their leaves stretched toward the sky, and how their shadows fell on the ground.

I was still seeing the same world, but my thinking had changed, so I saw things that I hadn't seen before.

And this is exactly what happens with opportunities.

The definition of opportunity is: "A set of circumstances that makes it possible to do something."

When it comes to doing what you love, there are no perfect sets of circumstances.

Doris Lessing, novelist and poet, put it well when she said: "Whatever you're meant to do, do it now. The conditions are always impossible."

Whenever you tell yourself that you can't do something because of your circumstances, it's a choice. Not something that is forced upon you, but chosen by you. We all have reasons for why we can't do what we love.

Kids. Work. No time. No talent. No ideas.

You could come up with a long list of excuses. Everyone could. Because you get what you focus on.

Opportunities are determined by how you view your current circumstances. Opportunity is not something you're given, but how you view the world. That view comes from inside of you.

While learning to draw, I could've resigned myself to the fact that I wasn't good. But I chose to keep going, and to keep using the skills I had. There were days when I made drawing harder than it should be by wishing I was someone else, someone who could draw photographically.

Once I relaxed into who I was, and what my skills were, the fog always lifted. When I stopped trying to bully my circumstances into place, things became easier. When I stopped wanting to be someone else, drawing became play again.

You may think you don't have the right set of circumstances to do what you love, but you do.

When you're inspired to do something, there's always a next step you can take.

The problem isn't that there isn't a step, but that you don't see it. Just like I began seeing new colors in the sky, so will you begin to see opportunities when you're willing to think small instead of big.

So how do you shift your perspective? You do what you can with what you have. If you can't take action on something, take action on what you can. It may not always be what you *think* it should be, but it will always be right in that moment.

Instead of looking at your circumstances as the enemy, look at it as your ally. Ask yourself: What am I supposed to learn here?

What if every moment is tailor-made to give you what you need in order to move forward?

You don't have to quit your job to write a book. You don't need a publishing deal to write. All that's required of you is one step at a time.

This has never been about opportunity. This is about what you're willing to do.

In one of my favorite books, *Accidental Genius*, Mark Levy writes: "I realized that if I was ever going to do anything that mattered with my life, I had to use whatever fixed mental and physical capacities I was born with. That is, unless I put in the effort, I wasn't going to suddenly become smarter, more athletic, or a greater success at anything."

Instead of focusing on what's wrong, focus on what you can do with what you have. You don't know if your circumstances are wrong. There's no way of telling. For all you know it may be exactly what you need right now.

Don't worry about picking the wrong opportunity. Opportunities are like trains. They come and go. If you miss one, you can catch another. Instead of looking for results and outcomes, look for learning opportunities.

While I spent a large part of my life not believing I could draw, I decided to change that by taking action and testing my assumptions. You can do the same.

Do what you can with what you have.

That's all that is required, because that's all that is possible.

Action Step

If you don't believe you have opportunities, you aren't thinking small enough. This isn't about book deals and silver platters. This is about being willing to start where you are.

If you pretended that life was exactly as it was supposed to be, what would you feel drawn to do next?

What can you do with what you have?

Start there. Start small.

On Challenges

Do you wonder why doing what you love isn't easier? Does it seem like whenever you are about to get started, something comes up? It could be a fear, an external obstacle, or just confusion.

Somewhere, somehow, we've learned that if we find what we love, find our calling, that life should be easy. Without problems.

The opposite is often true. When I do what I love, it seems as if I come up against more challenges. Instead of hiding from life, I'm following my heart, and sailing in uncharted waters.

That means I have to let go of old habits of thought, and old beliefs. You uncover these beliefs through living life, through taking action. When you look at a challenge, it's not truly a challenge. You give it that label because you think it stops you from getting what you want. For someone else, the same circumstance may not mean anything.

Challenges help reveal where your weaknesses lie, and what thoughts you believe that hold you back.

Challenge is merely change. And the word change means "to become." Each challenge then is a step in becoming more of who you are.

As Rumi puts it: "The moment you accept what troubles you've been given, the door will open."

Instead of shrinking away from challenges, use them to grow. Ask yourself: What am I learning here? What am I running away from? What am I scared of?

But remember to bring it back to the question: What tiny next step do I feel drawn to take?

See each challenge as a teacher, a teacher that reveals thoughts that have been holding you back. The fact that you are coming up against challenges means that you're taking action. It's a sign that you're on the right track. You're learning, growing, evolving.

There's nothing wrong with you if you don't succeed right away. Forget success. And bring yourself back to this moment. Notice that without a story, without thoughts, challenges could not exist, because a challenge is how we perceive something.

Often the most challenging time will be in the beginning. When I started going after what made my heart sing, it felt like I was invaded by my fears and insecurities. Just taking one step was exhausting. I was constantly second-guessing myself.

I knew that the thoughts weren't real, but they still had an impact. That's how it is sometimes. Luckily I had the resilience to keep going, despite the confusion.

As I did, my head began to clear. I began realizing, on a deep level, that I was okay.

I could do this.

No matter what challenge you face, you are okay. There is nothing that can hurt who you truly are. You are not your thoughts, your beliefs, or your accomplishments. You are that which experiences it all, the awareness in which thoughts originate.

No living being goes through life without facing challenges. A plant without challenges grows up weak.

Whenever I come upon a challenge, it's not the challenge that hurts me. It's my thinking. The moment I notice how I'm creating my experience, it's as if something lets go. It's not an effortful watching of my mind and letting go. It's a soft noticing, like watching birds sitting on a branch.

As you begin doing what you love, know that it's okay to bump into challenges. It simply means you're growing, and learning.

When you stop taking your thoughts so seriously, the frustration of challenges begins to fall away. Not completely, but it diminishes. I still wince when something goes wrong, but it's less and less as time goes by.

In the end, challenges help you do what you love. They mold you for what's to come. To quote Rumi again: "Where there is ruin, there is hope for a treasure."

What makes us suffer is our thinking. Some people see challenges as exciting learning opportunities, while others take them personally, thinking they aren't good enough if things don't go perfectly.

The difference is always in our thinking.

Action Step

Take something that you perceive to be an obstacle, challenge, or problem in your life, and consider the following question: What am I learning?

If you notice any thoughts of resisting the challenge, let them pass. Notice them. You don't have to entertain them. Nor do you have to control them. Let them be.

On Uncertainty

I was a professional poker player for half a decade. On a daily basis, I made decisions based on incomplete data. I received my cards. I studied my opponents. I knew the math. But many unknown factors remained.

A big unknown factor was luck. I could play perfect poker, but still come out in the red in the short-term. For example, in Texas Hold'em (what I played), I could get all my money in the middle being a 90% favorite, and still lose.

The same is true for doing what you love. It may seem like you're going nowhere from day to day, but as you look at yearly trends, you see that you're making progress.

You never have a complete view of what's going on. You have to do the best with what you have. Put another way: You have to be willing to guess, and take calculated risks.

A professional poker player knows the odds, and he knows how to play, but above all, he is in control of himself.

Many players may know how to play, but if they are off their game, they are more prone to making mistakes. They lose their edge against the other players at the table. A professional player can go from winner to loser in a heartbeat.

In life, if you're in a low mood, you're not fit to make decisions. You have to let yourself rest. When you push yourself, when you try to gain clarity where there is none, you exhaust yourself. Your moods are determined by your thoughts. And your thoughts always change. That means that, if you get out of the way, the mood will pass on its own.

While we want to control the future, that's not what this is about. External certainty doesn't exist, only internal certainty does. You can't control life, but you can control your reaction to it. You can control what thoughts you focus on, and how you approach life.

The future brings what it brings. You can only play life one hand, one moment, at a time, and then let the cards fall where they may.

As an entrepreneur and a writer, I struggle with uncertainty on a daily basis. I don't have a steady paycheck. What I do have is my internal certainty. I may not control my circumstances, and that's okay. Uncertainty is never the problem, only my thoughts about it.

For example, I cannot control the cards, but I can control my actions, and my decisions. I can make sure that I beat luck over the long-term. And the same is true in life. You cannot control life, but you can control your attitude. You can stay present and do your best.

Rumi once again comes to mind. He said: "Don't worry that your life is turning upside down. How do you know that the side you are used to is better than the one to come?"

If I'm truly honest with myself, I don't want complete certainty. Imagine a world where you knew what would happen. No unknown factors.

You might enjoy it for a day or two, but then it would become boring.

Lifeless.

Bland.

When put like that, wouldn't you rather have some uncertainty in your life and feel alive, rather than feel bored and lifeless?

We need the uncertainty. Without it there would be no possibility. There would be no comedy. No humor. No excitement.

How afraid you are of the future is dependent on what thoughts you pay attention to. I can think about ending up homeless, or I can focus on what I can do in this moment. It's a process of gently bringing back my mind to the here and now.

I bumped into this great quote from comedian Louis C.K.: "You'll be fine. You're 25. Feeling [unsure] and lost is part of your path. Don't avoid it. See what those feelings are showing you and use it. Take a breath. You'll be okay. Even if you don't feel okay all the time."

Even if you aren't 25 years old, it's relevant. It's okay to not feel okay. It's okay to not know everything. That's how it's supposed to be.

I don't know what will happen, and that's okay. Doing what you love is like playing poker. It's a journey of incomplete information, but that's what makes it so intriguing.

You never know what's coming next.

In the process, you learn to trust yourself.

To follow your inner wisdom.

To listen to your inner GPS.

Action Step

For this action step, I invite you to notice how uncertainty can be viewed in different ways.

Uncertainty isn't inherently bad. It's our thoughts about it that make us feel anything.

Uncertainty can be scary. Or it can make you curious. Interesting, isn't it?

On Overnight Success

Do you feel like you're not making progress fast enough? Do you see overnight success stories all over? Do they remind you of how you're not there yet?

You're not alone.

I've been there.

And still am from time to time.

What is overnight success? The stories you're told aren't the real stories. As Jonathan Fields, author of *Uncertainty*, writes: "Overnight success is really overnight exposure."

We see the exposure. We read the sensationalized story of how Twitter was born, or how a coach went from zero to seven-figures within a year.

What we don't see are the years of putting in the work, of trying and not quite getting it. We don't see that the coach building her skills prior to her breakthrough, prior to all the pieces of the puzzle falling together.

A big obstacle for people who are high achievers is that they underestimate how long it takes to build a business, do what you love, publish a book, or whatever it is you want to do.

For example, J.K. Rowling said that she wrote her first story when she was five or six. That's almost thirty years before the first Harry Potter book was published.

Adrian Brody, the famous actor, said: "My dad told me, 'It takes fifteen years to be an overnight success,' and it took me seventeen and a half."

When you dive deeper into the stories of successful people, you uncover the truth:

Overnight success does not exist. Not in the way it is portrayed.

Whatever you want to do in life, it will take time. Chances are you won't be an overnight sensation. Talent won't suddenly arrive and catapult you to the stars.

It sounds pessimistic when put like this, but to me this is a good thing. The problem isn't that you're not making progress fast enough, it's that you think you *should* be. It's easy to get caught up in the story that you're somehow doing something wrong.

As Debbie Millman said: "Expect anything worthwhile to take a long time."

Our expectations are the culprits. And you know what I'm going to say next, don't you? It's our thoughts. Expectations are simply thoughts about what we think the future will be. When those expectations aren't met, we have thoughts about not being enough. And we think we have to believe them, when we don't.

When I began following my heart, and doing what I love, I felt like I should've been more successful than I was. I constantly wondered what was wrong with me. I was angry at others. I was jealous, because I deserved more, I thought.

Looking back, I never needed more than I had. I was fine. The only things making me miserable were the thoughts I took seriously.

When you believe that overnight success is an option, and it doesn't happen, you look for what's wrong with you.

Misery is the result.

It has nothing to do with you, and everything to do with the ideas you have about success. When you think you don't measure up, you feel bad.

In the end, there's no measuring up to do. It's all going on inside your head. You becoming successful won't give you long-lasting happiness. How do I know? Look at the rich and famous. Some of them are happy. Some of them aren't.

You may need to work at a 9-to-5 job for a while. Or you may not. I don't know. What I do know is that you're always doing your best. (Even when you think you aren't). And that's enough.

You can only do what you do.

You can only keep showing up.

Success may come, or it may not. It doesn't really matter when you truly look at it. What matters is you doing what you love, as best you can, one moment at a time.

Action Step

How has the idea of overnight success been holding you back until now?

Explore your ideas around it. Notice how some of them make you miserable. And notice that they are thoughts you've picked up from outside of yourself.

Become aware of the relief of letting them go, of knowing that you don't have to purchase those thoughts in the marketplace of ideas. You can pass them by, and enjoy the scenery.

On Practice

The flip side of overnight success is practice. The more skills you accumulate, the more you can offer the world.

Practice is nothing more than taking steps on a daily basis to grow. To learn more. Often that means making mistakes, and learning from them. Sometimes it means taking a course, reading a book, or working with a coach. Above all, it means taking what you've learned so far, and putting it to practice.

You may not have all the skills you need, but that doesn't mean you can't help one person. I may not be a culinary chef, but I can still feed my son, and have a good time.

As Robert Greene writes in *Mastery:* "The biggest obstacle to becoming great at something is impatience. If you're in a rush, you want to skip the basics and jump to the prize right away, but it doesn't work like that. You have to put in the time if you want to become good, and if you want to see results... Learn to love learning. Learn to love the process of showing up every day to practice. This is the path."

As I've read about practicing, I've read about writers, artists, and entrepreneurs, who wake up at certain times, and do certain things, no matter how they feel. And while that seems to work great for some, it doesn't work for me. Not always.

Practicing doesn't necessarily mean sticking to a rigid schedule. But it does consist of you showing up and doing the work.

For example, I love writing. People ask me how I've developed my writing. The answer is simple: I've read a lot, and I've written a lot.

I've never had a rigid practice of writing a certain amount of words. I've simply shown up, and I've put words on paper. Sometimes I've written articles. Sometimes I've created courses. Writing has been the symptom of following my heart. Writing is how I express myself.

This doesn't mean I don't have days where I don't want to write, because I do. One of the aspects of practicing is realizing that it's not all rainbows and unicorns.

My practice includes writing, but also facing challenges, and noticing thoughts that hold me back. I'm afraid, and I worry. But once I get out of my own way, things seem to fall into place.

On the days where the whole world seems to be against me, I do my best, and I try to give myself plenty of breaks. I know that it's a mood that'll pass. I realize that when I'm in a low mood, I create problems that don't exist. The solution is not to fix things, but let the mood pass.

There's a hidden assumption there as well. It's this: I have to feel good to write well. And that isn't true. Sometimes amazing things come out of my fingertips when I'm having a bad day.

It comes down to showing up.

I don't want to give you another formula to follow. My practice changes, sometimes on a daily basis. So will yours.

What's constant in my life is the willingness to listen to my heart, to my inner wisdom, and take steps in the direction that feels magnetic to me. I go with the current of life.

While a rigid schedule doesn't work for me, it may work for you. The ideas in this book are meant to help you look inside for your answers. To find out for yourself.

When you do, you can respond to what the moment requires. You don't have to rely on the past to live your life. One day you may need a rigid schedule. One day you might not. When you listen to your heart, you'll know what to do. And when you don't, you'll do your best, and that'll be okay, too.

At its core, practicing is about learning, and becoming better. Developing skills takes time. I'm not the best writer in the world, but that doesn't mean I can't write. Sometimes I hate my writing, but I know it's just a thought. I keep writing.

I keep putting my work out there.

And I keep learning.

In a way, doing what you love is simply showing up every day, and doing your best. Whether you're in a job you don't like doesn't matter.

It's not about trying to become good enough. It's about realizing that you are good enough now, but that you still need to develop your skills.

As you take action, and make mistakes, you learn. Don't get stuck in trying to learn everything. Learn enough, then start.

Develop your own experiences.

Find what works for you.

Action Step

Consider the following question: What skills do you need, and want, to develop to do what you love?

Think in terms of daily action steps. Choose small daily habits, that when cultivated, naturally move you forward.

On Making Money

Do you worry about how you're going to turn what you love into something profitable?

Maybe you can't see how you're going to make a living doing what you love. Maybe you don't think you're good enough to charge for what you know.

To make money doing what you love, you need to help a real person with a real problem. Forget about helping thousands. Focus on helping just one person.

The problem most people run into—myself included—is that we think success should happen faster than it does. The truth is that it takes time to discover what you're good at, and what people want to pay you for.

The problem again isn't outside, but inside. It's the way you think about money, and business, that stops you.

You have thoughts that you've picked up from your parents, friends, and society. Someone else might have a different set of thoughts, so they take action right away.

To start making money doing what you love, start tiny. Don't worry about making $1,000 per month if you haven't made your first dollar. Focus on making your first $10 instead. Then your first $100.

As Lao Tzu said: "Great acts are made up of small deeds."

So how do you make your first dollar if you haven't already? Shift your spotlight onto the people you can help. Instead of thinking about how you can make money, ask yourself: How can I help?

At first, it may simply mean creating something simple and putting it out there. You could create a blog, a video, a podcast, or offer your services locally.

Sometimes you may not even see how you can help. All you know is that you feel excited about doing something. In that case, follow your excitement, and see what happens.

Learning to make money is a skill like anything else. It's not a faucet you turn on when you're thirsty. It's a skill you cultivate. You learn what people respond to. You learn to sell yourself and your ideas in an authentic way.

Again, there are no formulas to follow, even though many might want you to believe that there is.

You alone must uncover your own path. You do that by following your inner wisdom. Your inner wisdom will plop ideas into your head when you relax. We get our best ideas when we aren't thinking about our problems.

So ask yourself the question: How can I take the next step?

Then let it go.

The answer will come to you when the time is right. There is nothing you have to do about it, because that's how things work.

I get my best ideas when I'm taking a walk, sitting in the sauna (I live in Finland), playing with my son, or reading a good book.

Ideas come from nowhere.

There's nothing I can do to force them to emerge. When I relax, I get inspirational nudges, messages from my wisdom. But I have to allow myself to calm down, to not try to force things. When I don't get ideas, it's just a reminder that there's nothing to be done at that moment.

Avoid falling into the trap of prioritizing money. I've made this mistake many times. If I do something just to make money, it rarely works out. When I follow my heart, and do what I enjoy doing, while being practical, I'm on the right track.

If you need money fast, get a job. There's nothing wrong with using a job to support your path. If it's needed, then it's needed.

If there's anything I'd want to tell the Henri starting out, it's this: Take it easy. Don't try to force results. Don't compare yourself to others. Forge your own path. Listen to your inspiration. And be willing to start small.

That reminds me of a quote from Derek Sivers, entrepreneur and author, who once said: "Starting small puts 100% of your energy on actually solving real problems for real people. It gives you a stronger foundation to grow from."

Let it be okay to start with what you have, where you are. There's no need to be anywhere but right here.

You have what you need to take the next step.

You always do.

Action Step

Consider the following question: How can I help?

What does your heart yearn for? Who do you want to help? We have stories. We have experiences. There is always someone you can help.

It doesn't matter how insignificant you may think it is. Even a simple blog post can change someone's life. I know, because I've seen it happen.

On Running Away

There's something about doing what you love that makes me, and many people, want to run away—to hide from the world.

But I've noticed that it's not the world I want to hide from, but my own thoughts. It's never the world that makes me feel anything, because I'm always feeling my thinking.

I may be worried about putting myself out there, or being criticized, or failing. The truth is that I'm not worried about any of those things. I'm worried about the thoughts about those things.

So we run away not from our fears, and not from the outside world, but from ourselves. The irony is that we can never run far enough, because wherever we go, there we are.

Being a writer and an entrepreneur, I put myself out there on a daily basis. There are days when all I want to do is hide.

However, deep down, I know that escaping isn't going to make me happy. It's facing my fears, and living life to the fullest, that brings true fulfillment.

I want to live life.

Not hide.

It's when I'm having a bad day that I want to hide. But bad days, and low moods, are simply signs that I can't trust my thinking. I don't make good decisions when I feel bad. When I'm having a bad day, I try to give myself a break. If I can't, I do the best I can, and I try not to make big decisions.

And to quote Jack Pransky from his book *Somebody Should Have Told Us*: "Our feelings and emotions are our ready-available guides. Their purpose is to tell us whether our thinking is on or off track of our Health and well-being."

What underlies all of my running away is the thought that life should be easy. I assume that if I'm doing what I love, I shouldn't run into any obstacles. But it doesn't work that way.

If you want to do what you love, you have to be willing to grow. You have to stretch the boundaries of your comfort zone.

You could say that life is inherently difficult. It's difficult, but struggling is optional. Struggling comes from our thinking.

"It shouldn't be like this."

"Why did this happen to me."

"I'll never make it."

Those are thoughts we can entertain, or let be.

As Epictetus, Greek sage and Stoic philosopher, said: "People are disturbed, not by things, but the view they take of them."

While I may want to run away, I also know that it's not my job to map out my path. It's my job to take the next step. To use what I have in the best way I know how.

I've been repeating this throughout the book. There's a reason for that. This is what I've found to work. And when I repeat things from different angles, it increases the chances that you will remember and apply this information.

Without risk, there is no life. Saying no to risk means saying no to some of life's biggest pleasures: Love, friendship, family, art, and doing what you love.

People who do what they love, and live the life of their dreams, aren't fearless. They know that just because they have a thought, a fear, doesn't mean they have to listen to it.

While you may want to run away from doing what you love, know that it's not doing what you love you want to run away from, but the thoughts you have about it.

You don't have to figure everything out.

You don't have to know where you're going.

You simply have to bring your focus back to the present moment, and take the next tiny step.

Action Step

Here's a question for you to ponder: What scares you most about doing what you love?

Imagine that you get everything you want, that everything goes according to plan. You're doing what you love. You're making a difference.

Do you notice any resistance to this? Explore it. See what comes up.

On Synchronicity

One evening, we were driving home from an evening at my parents' house, and a song came on the radio. I don't normally pay too much attention to lyrics, but this time the words seemed to demand my attention.

The words came dancing out the speakers: "Take a look at the life you lead. What you got is all you need."

It was a song by Michael Monroe. The last part kept repeating itself: "What you got is all you need. What you got is all you need."

This came at a time when I was worrying about the future. I was stuck in my own thinking. Hearing the lyrics reminded me to take a look at my life. I did indeed have everything I needed to do what I loved to do.

It was my grasping for security that was causing problems. This synchronicity helped me notice that.

Synchronicity is akin to the universe leaving clues for me, nudging me in a certain direction. I'll know the event is relevant to me because my heart will feel open. The synchronicity arrives with a good, calm feeling

A book will show up at exactly the right time.

I'll overhear a conversation that sparks an idea.

Or taking action will lead me to an unexpected destination.

I don't understand how synchronicity works, but I don't have to know. All I have to do is listen to my heart. The more I've been willing to follow my   heart,   the   more   these   meaningful coincidences have shown up in my life. Or in other words, the more I've noticed them.

That's one of the reasons I try not to think too much about where I'm going. I have an idea, a direction, for where I'm going, but when I'm following my heart, there's no telling where I'll end up. As long as I follow the positive pulls of my being, I know I'll end up where I need to be.

It seems that there's a force larger than me at play, orchestrating my movements. You could call this force God, Allah, the Universe, energy. To me it's all the same thing, an intelligence wanting to express itself through me, through all of us.

Because who am I? I'm made out of this earth. I am the stars, and the planets. Where does my being come from? I don't know, but I feel it. I feel that I'm beyond just this body.

There's a lot I don't know. But it doesn't stop me from marveling at the mystery of life. I'm not here to figure it all out.

I'm here to live it.

To enjoy the ride.

Synchronicity is not something I engineer consciously. I go about my life. I follow my heart, I get out of my own way, and it shows up.

It's already happening in your life. The question is: Are you paying attention?

I don't mean pay attention in a frantic way, but relaxed awareness of the fact that the world around you has something to tell you, like the song on the radio telling me that everything was okay.

Watch out for forcing synchronicity. It's easy to give something in your life meaning, sometimes without even knowing it.

This is where gaining experience comes in. Pay attention. Some clues will be false (made up by yourself) and others will be surprising, nudges from something deeper, something beyond you.

Your life is filled with meaningful coincidences. Don't take my word for it. Go out there, and see for yourself.

For all I know, I could be fabricating synchronicity. But it wouldn't matter to me. The results are the same: Happiness, growth, and living the life I want to live.

When you start doing what you love—when you commit to following your heart—it's as if the universe starts cooperating.

But you have to be willing to take the first step.

Action Step

It's easy to forget how big of an impact coincidences have on our life. For example, look at the biggest events in your life. They weren't under your control. You didn't consciously manipulate them into place.

I invite you to explore the following question: What are three meaningful coincidences you've run into in your life?

Look at what had to be in place for them to happen. I think you'll be surprised to discover how unlikely they were.

When you're done, turn the page.

On Finding Your Path

Finding my path in life hasn't been easy. I always thought I needed to look outside of myself to be on the right track. I thought I needed someone else to tell me that I was moving in a direction that would make me happy.

But what does finding your path mean? To me it means living from my heart. Being in touch with my wisdom. Noticing where life wants to take me, where I feel pulled to go.

It's as if I'm not living life—I'm moved by life.

Mystics, masters, and teachers have been pointing to this for thousands of years. Even scientists know that at the molecular level, we're all the same, and we're all connected.

Within me, and within you, there is an intelligence, an inner wisdom, waiting to guide us, if we're willing to calm down and listen.

You already have the guidance you need within you. What's obscuring it is thinking. Trying to figure life out. Trying to control. Trying to analyze everything.

Finding your path in life simply means letting this inner wisdom guide you. The way you do that is by doing nothing at all. You stop trying.

This doesn't mean you stop doing anything in life. It means you stop trying mentally. When your mind calms down, your wisdom is there. Just like the sun is always there, no matter what the weather is like.

When you try to live life logically, you end up messing things up. Now, following your wisdom doesn't mean that you'll make perfect decisions, because who can really know what a perfect decision is? We can't predict the future, which means we don't know where something will lead.

The way I live life today is to respond to whatever life presents. This is different from merely reacting to life. I trust that I know what to do. I trust my inner wisdom.

It's like Virginia Woolf put it: "Arrange whatever pieces come your way."

In a way, you're already on your path. You don't have to find something else. The seeking gets in the way of the answer. Everything you need is already within you.

Avoid taking action when you're in a negative state of mind. When you feel bad, your mind will create problems, and there will be a sense of urgency to act. That sense of urgency comes from an insecure thought. It's a sign that you need a break, and that your thinking cannot be trusted.

When a thought comes from your inner wisdom, it comes with an uplifting feeling. It might feel joyous, calm, free, relaxed, or some other positive feeling. Listen and notice how your inner wisdom communicates with you.

When I began living from my wisdom, it didn't make sense to my mind. But I was open to it, because I knew that living a life based solely on logic wasn't the answer.

I don't know where I'm going. I only know where I'm feeling pulled this moment. There's a sense of freedom in letting go of all the trying to control.

Doing what I love has been about listening to my wisdom, and living my truth. Instead of looking outside for the answers, I look inside. I follow what feels magnetic to me.

That's it.

I still read books. I take in information. But I try to only take in what feels magnetic to me.

That's what I've spent this whole book pointing toward—the wisdom that is within all of us, and how we use our thinking to fool ourselves.

So instead of you trying to mold life to the way you think it *should* be, let life unfold through you.

Joseph Campbell put it well when he said: "We must let go of the life we have planned, so as to accept the one that is waiting for us."

It's not your job to figure life out. You know this because when you try, you become frustrated and overwhelmed.

I'm not saying don't plan. I'm saying be aware of when you're forcing yourself to do something you don't need to do.

Become quiet, and listen to the wisdom that is already within you.

It will guide you through life.

You don't have to find your path, because you're already on it.

Action Step

If you've never listened to your inner wisdom, writing can be a great way to re-connect. But remember, you've never really lost the connection. Your wisdom is always within you, because it is you.

To notice the connection that is already there, explore the following question: What does my inner wisdom want to tell me, right now?

If you feel stuck, try dumping your mind on paper first. Write whatever comes to mind for 10-15 minutes. Then ask the question.

On Getting Started

We've covered a lot of ground, and we've reached the final chapter. I want to end this book by getting you focused on moving forward.

Most of the people I work with already know enough to take the next step. What's holding them back are thoughts like:

"I don't know what to do."

"I don't know enough."

"I have too many interests."

"I can't see the next step."

When you're willing to start small, to start tiny, you can start today. Forget about writing a best-selling book, and write a 100-word blog post. Create a 1-minute video. Sell a tiny course.

When you think in tiny steps, your brain doesn't freak out. When your mind wants to think about the future, gently bring it back to the present moment. Remember that all you have to do is your best. Listen to your inner wisdom, and take the next smallest step.

If you can't take action on something, take action on what you can. The path you think will lead you to your destination is rarely the one you end up taking. I say this from personal experience.

I've noticed that when I do what I can, and I follow my wisdom, things tend to work out. This doesn't mean they always work out, but I feel like I'm on the right track. I'm doing what I can.

If you're stuck, it's never that you're truly stuck, but that you're believing unhelpful thoughts. You can always take one tiny step in some direction.

Once you start moving, you realize that you don't know where you're going. You don't know how life works. No one truly does. We live in a mystery. And that mystery is lived one moment at a time.

As Austin Kleon, author of *Steal Like an Artist* and *Show Your Work*, writes: "Don't wait until you know who you are to get started. The way you figure yourself out is by making things."

Most books try to give you a formula. They truly want to help. But giving you a formula would be a disservice to you, because it would mean that I knew more about your life than you do.

No one can live your life for you. No one can tell you what you're passionate about. You have to be willing to trust your inner wisdom, and travel your path.

You may feel scared. You may be worried. You may not know what you're doing. But that's okay. That's just a sign that you're doing something new.

You don't have to have everything figured out.

In fact, you can't.

All you have to do is listen to that voice within you.

If you ever feel like you can't hear that voice, don't worry. I find that when I'm in a low mood, I have trouble as well. What I do is wait. I don't try to force it. I simply do my best.

I've kept repeating this over and over again, but let me say it again: All you have to do is what you can with what you have, where you are. That is enough.

Sometimes I don't hear my inner wisdom. Sometimes I do. Nevertheless, I try to stay in the present moment, and do my best.

I again want to remind you to not take my words as truth.

Put what you've learned in this book to the test.

Start listening to your heart, to your wisdom. Start doing what you love.

It's not going to be a panacea. It's going to be the start of a new way of living life.

Action Step

Since this is the last chapter, I invite you to close your eyes, and just be.

Relax your body, and your mind for ten seconds. Let every idea, worry, fear, and concept be. Let your thoughts be.

Relax everything.

Just be.

Final Words

My aim with this book has been to nudge you to look inside, and to help you see that nothing is holding you back, except your thoughts.

That doesn't mean taking action is easy. It often isn't. It means that the possibility always exists for you.

Whatever we think, we experience. We live life through our thoughts. That's why no one has the exact same experience of life.

Remember that there is no rush. No rush to become someone, or achieve something. Take this journey at your own pace.

Listen to your own heart. Take breaks. Be present. Take time off to do what you enjoy. When your mind clears, the answers will come to you, because that's how this works.

You already know how to do what you love. What stops you is thinking that you have to do something a certain way.

You don't have to figure life out. You don't have to plan (unless you want to). You simply have to become quiet, and look to your inner wisdom, the stillness within you.

As you do, the next step will become clear. If it doesn't, be still for a moment. Then if you feel like taking action, and you still don't know, any step will do.

As Antonio Machado, Spanish poet, said:

"Traveler, your footprints
are the only road, nothing else.
Traveler, there is no road;
you make your own path as you walk.
As you walk, you make your own road,
and when you look back
you see the path

you will never travel again.
Traveler, there is no road;
only a ship's wake in the sea."

This book has been about my story, and my experiences.

Now it's your turn to use what you've learned, and make it your own.

A Request

I'm not a big publishing company. I'm one guy writing books, hoping to help people wake up to the fact that they can do what they love.

That's why I want to ask you to spread the word about this book (if you liked it), and leave a review on Amazon. Or if you're on platforms like Goodreads, you can review it there as well.

Anything you can do is appreciated.

Books

If you're interested in reading more from me, I have two books that fit well with this one. They are:

Find Your Passion: 25 Questions You Must Ask Yourself

Follow Your Heart: 21 Days to a More Fulfilling Life

Whatever you decide, allow yourself to take a break after reading this book. Don't rush for more information. Instead, return inside, and let the next step come to you.

Connect

If you'd like to learn more about me, and how to do work you love, come visit me at: http://www.wakeupcloud.com/

I have a free newsletter that I think you'd enjoy. When you join, you get a free report and audiobook on how to make a living doing what you love.

You'll also get content on a weekly basis that helps you move toward making money following your passion.

To join the newsletter, go to: http://www.wakeupcloud.com/newsletter/

If you have any questions, comments, find broken links, or just want to say hi, feel free to email me at: henri@wakeupcloud.com.

Resources

I always get asked about relevant resources, so here's a short list of what I recommend after you've read this book. (The list below also includes books mentioned in this book).

The Inside-Out Revolution **by Michael Neill** - This is a fantastic book about the inside-out nature of life. If you'd like to learn more about how we experience life, I highly recommend this book. It's short, and to the point.

Somebody Should Have Told Us **by Jack Pransky** - This is another book that covers how our thoughts create our moment to moment experiences. I recommend this book after you've read *The Inside-Out Revolution*.

***Steal Like an Artist* by Austin Kleon** - This is a fun little book that reminds you of the fact that you don't have to come up with groundbreaking ideas. You just have to steal, and put in the work.

***Show Your Work* by Austin Kleon** - Another short book from Austin Kleon. This one is about getting your work out in the world. A good book if you don't see yourself as the sales-y type.

***Mastery* by Robert Greene** - This book is a heavier read than the above, but I still enjoyed reading Robert Greene's take on the topic. Highly recommended book. Just take it one bite at a time.

***Live Your Truth* by Kamal Ravikant** - This is a short book telling Kamal's story through short essays. It's a quick read, but enlightening. Kamal is a great writer, and a great person.

The Art of Being Unmistakable (http://www.unmistakablecreative.com/) - If you're not a fan of reading, this is a great podcast where Srinivas Rao interviews entrepreneurs, creatives, and authors from all walks of life. It's inspirational, empowering, and filled with insights.

And remember, there's plenty of free articles and videos over at my website (http://www.wakeupcloud.com/).

See you there!